Bray in Old Photographs

Arthur Flynn

GILL & MACMILLAN

To Garrett and Anna

Gill & Macmillan Ltd
Hume Avenue, Park West, Dublin 12
with associated companies throughout the world
www.gillmacmillan.ie
© Arthur Flynn 2004
0 7171 3618 3
Design and print origination by O'K Graphic Design, Dublin

Printed in Malaysia

This book is typeset in Caslon 540 and Cochin.

The paper used in this book comes from the wood pulp of managed forests. For every tree felled, at least one tree is planted, thereby renewing natural resources.

A CIP catalogue record for this book is available from the British Library.

1 3 5 4 2

Contents

Acknowledgments

I owe a debt of appreciation to many people without whose help and advice I could not have completed this book. I would like to begin by acknowledging the assistance of my extended family and friends. I would also like to thank Peter Regan, Michael O'Brien, Gertie Allen, John Byrne, Jim and Angela Molloy, Sister Sheila, Sister Josephine, Irene Ledwidge, Anne Windsor, Brian White, Fr John O'Connell, Frank Loughrey, Vaughan Dodd, Kathleen Kinsella, Henry Cairns, Bruce Chandler, Bridgie and Sean Fox, Joan Codyre, Mary Forde, Carol Hannay, Hedley Wright, Séamus Reynolds, Paul O'Toole, John Smith, Jackie Napier, John Doyle, Nuala and Jim Tobin, Jimmy O'Toole, Séamus Flynn, Ita McGarry, Derek Pullin, Joe Behan, Maura McGahon, Padraig Doyle, Robert Butler and Noelle Ringwood Ballywaltrim Library, Michael Kelleher and Tom French Bray Library, Dermot de Barra Bray Tourism, Michael O'Brien, Michael Fortune, Aileen Parle, Maria Brunton, Michael Duffy, Bray Wanderers and Bray Emmets. I apologise if I have omitted anybody's name.

A special word of thanks to Noel Rowsome for advice on the technology and to Damian for assistance with research. I would also like to thank my wife Geraldine who provided me with unstinting support.

Introduction

B ray is situated twelve miles south of Dublin, in an area of great natural beauty. The town is located on either side of the Dargle River, framed to the east by the sea, south by the bulk of Bray Head and west by the Sugarloaf and Wicklow Mountains. The sea-front and promenade still maintain an element of Victorian charm.

It is believed that the name Bray evolved from the clan name of Uí Briuin Cualann. Old church records refer to the town as Bré, indicating that it may have derived its name from the Gaelic word *brí* (hill or rising ground), a reference to Bray Head and the many steep inclines throughout the town.

The ancient church sites that surround the town bear witness to its historic past, but an even older aspect is the pre-historic feature of Bray Head, with its area of Cambrian rocks dating to between 200 and 500 million years ago. More evidence of the town's ancient past lies in the submerged primeval forest at the north beach, which has a radiocarbon age of 6,750 years.

In the late eighth century the Vikings established a small settlement in Bray from which they launched raids on the monasteries of north Wicklow.

In 1173, following the Anglo-Norman invasion, King Henry II granted the manor of Bré to the Norman knight, Sir Walter de Ridelisford. De Ridelisford built the great feudal castle of Bré on high ground near the present bridge. For two centuries the Irish clans, the O'Tooles and the O'Byrnes, repeatedly raided the town. In 1313 they attacked the castle, and the lands around Bray lay waste for many years. In 1402 a fierce battle was fought near Ravenswell in which the septs and citizens of Dublin defeated a force of O'Byrnes. Four hundred were slain in the encounter.

One of the finest houses in County Wicklow is Killruddery House, on the outskirts of the town, home of the Brabazon family for over four centuries. In 1545 King Henry VIII granted the lands, once owned by monks, to Lord Brabazon. They were benevolent landlords and provided a fever hospital, infirmary, town hall and market house for the community.

By 1700 Bray had become a medium-sized fishing and market town where the poor of Little Bray lived in deplorable conditions in one-roomed mud cabins. The area was frequently flooded and in 1741 the bridge was washed away in a fierce storm. The only industries existing at that time were brewing, distilling and milling. By the 1770s coaches were running through Bray en route from Dublin to Wexford. Quin's Hotel (now the Royal Hotel) was one of many hotels that opened to accommodate travellers.

The coming of the railway to Bray in 1845 was to change the fortune of the town. The combination of the railway and the Victorian belief in the beneficial effects of seawater transformed Bray into a fashionable resort. Large villas and terraces were built along the sea-front. New roads were developed, many given royal names — Albert Walk, Prince of Wales Terrace and Victoria Avenue.

An enterprising businessman named William Dargan was to develop the town further, building the impressive Turkish Baths (which were unceremoniously demolished), Quinsboro Road and the promenade, deservedly earning the town the title, the 'Brighton of Ireland'. The railway line was later extended under Bray Head and onwards to Wicklow town.

The project of compiling this book presented me with a challenge and involved much research and detective work. In the most unlikely places I discovered treasure troves of nostalgia. Long-forgotten faded photographs were produced from dusty attics, from under beds and tattered albums. What began as a trickle turned into a flood, and I was soon snowed under with a mound of valued photographs. My problem soon became one of what to omit rather than what to include.

This book is not about the famous people who have had connections with the town, such as James Joyce, Oscar Wilde and Paul Henry, but the ordinary people at work and at play. Some photographs do not have the detail or sharpness of the Lawrence Collection, but I felt it important to include them for their individual social dimension.

Through the photographs I have attempted to trace Bray's changing face from the advent of the railway and subsequent new prosperity to the present sprawling commuter town. I have dipped into the social history of a past that is mainly lost in our rush towards progress. Included are box camera images of families, pets, friends, trips and events around them, creating a collective portrait of their society. Photographs produce a social-public memory by way of memoirs.

Pictorial records of several presidential visits to Bray are included. Cearbhall Ó Dálaigh, who was born in Bray, received a rapturous reception when he paid several official visits to the town as President.

Bray has a strong tradition of art and culture, and during the 1940s there were six drama groups active in the town. I have included some of their exciting productions, along with the St Kevin's Band, Bray Choral Society and the Bray Musical Society, who have provided their distinctive forms of entertainment for many decades.

No pictorial portrait of Bray would be complete without mention of the Eagle's Nest, Bar B and the Arcadia Ballrooms. For thousands of people over many generations they rekindle memories of Billy Carter and the showband era. Countless romances began in all of these venues. Alas this era has passed.

Another tradition relegated to an era of nostalgia is the annual Corpus Christi procession in which all the organisations throughout the town participated. I have included some photographs that should evoke those days.

Sport has always been a strong feature of life in Bray and I have been able to assemble the earliest records of some of its sporting heroes. Soccer is represented by Bray Wanderers and previously by Bray Unknowns, and the GAA by Bray Emmets and Camogie teams. Golf and water sports are also popular pastimes in Bray.

The family businesses of Tanseys, Regans, Colliers and Allens and many others weave a historical pattern of the commerce of the town, as they passed from generation to generation. Other photographs capture the contrasts of life from the grandeur of Killruddery to the humble homes of Little Bray. And no book on Bray would be complete without the inclusion of photographs from its film-making tradition.

The elements must feature prominently in any profile of Bray as for centuries the sea and river have been friends and foes to the people. I have attempted to capture the extreme contrasts, from children frolicking in the sea, to leisurely strolls on the prom, to the disastrous floods which have struck the sea-front and Little Bray areas. On the flip side many generations have enjoyed a variety of sea sports: sailing, rowing, swimming and fishing.

Now that the town has become a dormitory base for Dublin, hopefully this book will give newcomers an insight into Bray's past. With a population of over 27,000, it is the largest town in County Wicklow and one of the most important on the east coast. I hope I have captured the diversity of life in the town over the past 150 years.

1

Sights and Scenes

Turkish Baths, c. 1910

In 1859 the businessman William Dargan built the Turkish Baths on Quinsboro Road. In 1867 they were converted into the Assembly Rooms where concerts were staged. Later the building was transformed into McDermott's Picture House. In 1981 the building was demolished to make way for a shopping centre.

The White Coons, c. *1926*

The White Coons were one of the most popular performing groups in Bray in the early 1900s. They performed their singing and dancing routines on the smaller of the two bandstands, opposite the Esplanade Hotel. There was no charge, but at the end of each show the hat would be passed around amongst the eager audience.

The White Coons, c. *1926*
The White Coons in a formal pose.

Little Bray Castle, c. 1918

The exact date of the erection of this castle in Little Bray is not known but it appears on the Down Survey map of 1657. This castle is believed to have been erected to guard a ford across the Dargle River. It was demolished *c.* 1938.

Old Court Castle, c. 1910

Old Court Castle, originally known as Mulso's Castle, was built in 1429 by an English knight Sir Thomas Mulso. Later the castle passed into the possession of the Walshes of Carrickmines. It is still standing today.

Killruddery House, **c. 1930**

In 1545 Sir William Brabazon received a grant of land from Henry VIII; this included the lands of Killruddery at the yearly rent of £8.6s.8d, together with two foot-soldiers for the defence of the property. The Brabazons were the most influential family in the town for four and a half centuries. In 1627 they became the Earls of Meath and built Killruddery House in 1682. William and Richard Morrisson were commissioned to redesign the building in 1820, and further renovations were carried out in 1952 due to dry rot.

Killruddery Gardens, **c. 1945**

Killruddery House is surrounded by extensive gardens, some over 300 years old. Situated to the south of the house are the seventeenth-century gardens comprising the Angles, the Long Ponds, the Sylvan Theatre and the Beech Hedge Pond. Sir Walter Scott attended a performance at the Sylvan Theatre.

Killruddery Gardens, **c. 1888**
A garden party in the grounds of the house, hosted by Lord and Lady Meath, with the band of the Boys Brigade.

Total Abstinence Association, c. 1901

A section of the large attendance at the Total Abstinence Association gathering at Crinken. Note the number of priests and nuns amongst the congregation, including the Sisters of Charity with their distinctive head dresses, which earned them the name of 'God's Geese'.

Ladies Concert, c. 1895

A concert for a ladies group at the bathing pavilion on Bray Esplanade.

2

Sea-front

Martello Tower, c. 1880

A coastal view with the number one Martello tower clearly visible on the shoreline. It was situated close to where the cockbrook flowed into the sea. This tower was demolished in the 1880s. The second tower above the harbour still stands as a private residence. The third tower at the rear of Ravenswell Convent collapsed into the sea in the 1860s.

Naylor's Cove, c. 1905

The photograph shows the swimming boxes at Bray Cove Baths. The baths were a hub of activity where water polo matches and swimming galas were held. In 1900 a railway platform was constructed above the cove, and people could make their way down to the baths on foot. Until 1930 there were separate changing and bathing areas for males and females.

Bray Promenade, c. 1901

This is a postcard sent from Bray to Moville, County Donegal. At that time Bray was known as the 'Brighton of Ireland' and people travelled from all over the country to holiday there.

Bray Regatta, c. *1920*

One of the biggest attractions on the seashore during the summer months was the annual regatta. Teams from Ringsend, Bulloch and Wicklow would participate against local teams. Hundreds of enthusiastic spectators would travel to Bray and line the promenade to watch the activities and cheer on their teams.

Bray Regatta, c. *1920*

Another view of the regatta. Note the heavy clothing of the spectators sitting on the stony beach, despite the sunny day.

Bray Prom, c. *1948*
A quiet scene of the esplanade with two happy couples enjoying the view. Midway along the right side is the Bray Head Hotel at the base of Bray Head.

Bray Beach, c. *1938*
A man unseasonably dressed in a trench coat and cap watches as his children play on the beach.

Bray Head, c. 1920

The eastern side of Bray Head clearly showing the railway line, and above it the Cliff Walk that links Bray to Greystones. In recent years coastal erosion has made this walk unsafe.

Beach, c. 1948

A sunny scene of boys and girls enjoying themselves beside the old pier. This pier was later wrecked during a storm. In 1935 Bray Urban District Council erected six kiosks along the esplanade and one at the base of Bray Head. These kiosks were let each summer as seasonal shops.

Swimmers, c. 1933
Male swimmers in the Kilmartin Cup dive from the harbour wall at the start of the race.

Stormy Sea, c. 1994
A deserted promenade takes a pounding from the sea. On occasion the car park to the right
has been littered with stones and pebbles which damaged cars with the force of the waves.

Stormy Sea, c. *1998*

This photograph shows the beginning of the Coastal Erosion Protection Scheme. The project, now completed, offers protection to the promenade but has ruined the appearance of the sea-front.

Bray Swans, c. *1999*

One of the biggest attractions in Bray harbour in recent years has been the swans. Their number has increased from two to 120 in ten years. In the photograph, two-year-old Ben Rowsome is followed by some friendly swans in search of food.

Sea-front, c. 1948

A scene which depicts Bray at the height of the summer season. People travelled by bus, train and car to enjoy the sea, the amusements and a range of dance halls, pubs and fish-and-chippers. Many houses throughout the town put up B&B signs to accommodate an overflow of visitors during the peak season.

Salvage, c. 1968

Children salvage driftwood and other debris following a storm at the harbour.

Young Swimmer, c. *1970*
This young boy appears to be proud of his catch of seaweed.

A Snowy Prom, c. *1963*
The sea-front cloaked in a blanket of snow. Note the old-style baths in the foreground. The Sea Life Aquarium and Barracuda Restaurant are now on this site.

Ban∂4tan∂, c. *1995*

A more recent, sunny photograph of the newly painted bandstand. In the summer months it is used for band recitals, concerts, dog shows, pop groups and various events during the Seaside Festival. The lights and flags which extend along the prom to the bottom of Bray Head add a festive air to the resort. The old fairy lights have been replaced by modern lighting.

Sewerage Work4, c. *1988*

Children explore the laying of sewage pipes at Bray Harbour. This major project involved the construction of the Sewerage Outfall Pipe for 1.5 miles out to sea from the new pumping station on Dock Hill.

Chair Lift, c. 1963
The aerial chairlift on Bray Head was erected in 1952 by Irish Holidays. It was a welcome addition to the amenities of the resort, and brought passengers from the base of Bray Head to and from the Eagle's Nest. The chairlift ran commercially until 1976.

Donkey Ride, c. 1937
Young Kathleen Corcoran enjoys a donkey ride on Bray beach. Pat Grant offers her some reassurances.

Happy Group, c. 1952
A lively group of boys and girls have fun astride a boat on Bray promenade.

3

Industry and Business

S. Byrne, c. 1930

From the 1920s for many decades, Byrnes of number 10 Main Street was one of the leading ladies' dress shops in the town. The photograph shows the staff standing by the door. In later years the shop was taken over by Gaffneys, another ladies' dress shop.

John Stuart, c. 1904

John Stuart, the family grocery premises, occupied a prime location at the junction of Main Street and Novara Road. Note the staff of the shop in their long white aprons and dresses. To the left of the shop are the delivery horses and carts.

Milk Delivery, c. 1940

Local farmer and milkman Frank McLoughlin on his milk delivery round at Bray Head Terrace. He had a small farm and herd of cows at Vevay Road.

Fishermen, c. 1920
Some veteran Bray fishermen proudly display their catch outside the Boat House.

O'Reilly's, c. 1910
An advertisement for O'Reilly's, Quinsboro Road, grocer and off-licence. Note the telephone number – 15 Bray. O'Brien's, the off-licence, now occupies that location.

O'REILLY & Cº.

HIGH-CLASS GROCERS, WINE, SPIRIT, TEA AND PROVISION MERCHANTS.

GENUINE VALUE! BEST BRANDS!
LOWEST PRICES!

NOTE THE ADDRESS:

Quinsboro' Road, BRAY.
TELEPHONE No. 15 BRAY.

Mick Napier, c. 1940
Mick Napier (right) and his assistant outside his barber's shop on Florence Road. This was one of many barbers in the town around this period.

Allen Family, c. 1915

(Front) Jack, Kathleen and Willie, (Back) Harry, Tom and Jim Allen of the well-known Bray drapery family. They ran the family business in Main Street for almost a century. The shop still trades today.

Tansey, c. 1920

Tansey & Company, number 20 Quinsboro Road, is another long-established drapery business in Bray. Note the packed window display of hats and shirts, and other items hanging over the windows. Tansey's still trades in the same location today.

Tansey, c. 1920

A newspaper advertisement on Saturday 30 May 1920 for Tansey & Company.

Regan's, c. 1953

Mary Regan stands at the door of her grocery shop at number 56 Main Street, with two young customers. The jars of boiled sweets in the left-hand window were manufactured in Kennymore Sweet Factory in Bray.

Pearce, c. 1890

The family grocery and tea-rooms of George Pearce at number 45 Main Street was located just below the Town Hall. Mr Pearce (in suit) and two of his staff stand outside the shop. The Bank of Ireland now occupies this premises.

Bray Painters, c. 1900

Nine members of the Bray Painters Union. Moustaches and caps were popular during this period.

Dustbin Men, c. 1959

This happy group of Bray bin men comprises John Byrne, Sammy Murray, George McCormack and John Murray. They are standing beside the lorry with the gasometer in the background. The Back Strand area was then used for dumping rubbish.

Maple, c. 1950

An advertisement for the Maple Ballroom, Maple Ice Cream Parlour and Kennymore Products. Kennymore were the manufacturers of hard sweets, cordials and fruit squashes. Their factory in Castle Street was one of the most popular places in the town to pass by and sniff the aroma of their mixes.

Pawnbroker, c. 1935
One of the staff of L. J. McKeown, pawnbroker, draper and jeweller, on Main Street, standing at the door.

Delivery, c. 1965
A delivery of Coca-Cola being brought up to the Eagle's Nest on the aerial railway.

Solus Teo, c. *1935*

The workers of Solus Teo, manufacturers of light bulbs at Corke Abbey, posing for a photograph. Some children were brought in for the occasion. The factory continues to thrive today.

Colliers, c. *1938*

Some of the staff of Colliers, the coffin-makers and undertakers in Little Bray. The company was originally established in 1837 as Miller's. From the late 1920s the company employed up to 140 people and transported coffins by rail all over Ireland. At one stage they had a contract to supply coffins to Gibraltar. The company is still trading at Old Connaught Avenue.

4

Social and Leisure

Variety Concert, c. 1925

The cast of dancers, singers, musicians and actors of a Variety Concert in the Florence Hall. During this period, an evening's entertainment consisted of a concert followed by a one-act play.

Lizzy Doyle, c. 1914
Lizzie Doyle and her children, Joe and Mary, of Seapoint Road.

Scor, c. 1972
Catherine Kirwan, Joe Kirwan, Jimmy Lyons and Seán Fox on stage during the Scor Competition in the Little Flower Hall.

Oriental Band, c. 1920
The eight-piece Oriental Band playing in the Arcadia Ballroom. They were one of the many bands who entertained dancers at this popular venue.

Bill Murphy's Ceilidhe Band, c. 1940

Bill Murphy's band played at ceilis and social events throughout Wicklow and the surrounding counties. The band members from left are: Terry Whelan, Seán Fox, Christy Ward, Jim Byrne, and Bill Murphy on accordion.

'Rosemarie', c. 1969

Bray Musical Society's production of 'Rosemarie'. Amongst those on stage are Jim Molloy, Father Byrne, Maureen Murphy, Bill McInerney and Jack Leonard. The Society was founded in 1952 and has produced a range of entertaining shows annually since then.

'The Boy Friend', c. *1989*

In high spirits on Bray sea-front is some of the cast of the Bray Musical Society's production of 'The Boy Friend'. Included are: Cathy Corcoran, Ann Murphy, Liz Anne Woollam, Fionnuala Kinsella, Yvonne Prendergast, Nuala McKenna, Tommy Reid, Dick McGahon, Conor McCabe, Martin Fehily and Denis Sherlock.

Nativity Play, c. *1952*

The cast of the Nativity play in the Florence Hall. For weeks before the opening, mothers were busy adjusting sheets and pillowcases for use as costumes.

Dog Show, c. *1910*
Participants in the annual dog show that took place on the sea-front.

Quadrille, c. *1906*
The committee of the Ivy Quadrille Class.

Gala Social, c. 1918
A large gala social gathering in the Arcadia Ballroom.

Cuala Theatre Group, 1947
Members of the Cuala Theatre Group on an outing to the Dargle Pool. (Left to right) Back: Hugh Jordan, Oliver Bradley, Colbert Martin, Dermot Murphy, Kathleen Keogh, Frank Kinsella and (?). Front: Leo Kinsella, Deirdre Robinson, Fiona Robinson, Tina Coates, Ann Nolan and Bernie Byrne.

Happy Group, c. 1932
A group of young people enjoying an evening out at Dawson's Amusements.

Soap Box Derby, c. 1953
Spectators and participants in the Bray Swimming Club Soap Box Derby gather outside the club house. The derby was one of the highlights of the club's activities.

Funfair, c. *1920*

A funfair on the southern slope of Bray Head. These were regular events during the summer months. Williams Amusement Park was also situated at this location. On occasions there were even open-air film shows.

An Toastal, c. *1953*

A children's fancy dress competition in the Arcadia Ballroom held as part of An Toastal festival. At the rear in glasses, Mr Hipwell. The two women in the centre are Irene Hynes and Miriam O'Byrne.

Bray Theatre Festival, c. 1946
From left, Joan McKay, winner in the Three-Act Play category, centre Ronald Ibbs, adjudicator and Kathleen Keogh, winner in the One-Act Play category. The competing plays were performed nightly in the Little Flower Hall.

Bray Choral Society, c. 1991
The Bray Choral Society giving a recital of Hayden's *Creation* in the Church of the Most Holy Redeemer.

Conway Family, c. 1949

Three generations of the Conway family in the garden of Kimberley, Upper Dargle Road. Seated right, Granny Elizabeth Conway. Beside her is daughter Gertie, and behind is her son Arthur Conway and his wife Amy. The children are grandchildren Art and Deirdre.

Play Competition, c. 1978

Members of the committee of the Bray One-Act Play Competition which has been running successfully in the Parochial Hall since 1977. From left, Brian Studdart, Fred Lee, Maeve Spotwood and Bruce Chandler.

Old Time Music Hall, c. 1967

The cast of the Old Time Music Hall relaxing between scenes at the International Hotel. Included in the cast are Mary Forde, C. Healy, C. Short, M. O'Sullivan, M. Hughes, M. O'Reilly, M. Nolan, Mrs Mustard, Mrs Gillen and two unknowns.

Social Gathering, c. *1980*
Members of the Orchard Nursing Home and the Bray Old Folks at one of their regular social events.

Girls, c. *1949*
Four happy, well-dressed girls posing in the grounds of Loreto Convent.

5

Sport

Bray Wanderers,* c. *1927

Bray Wanderers soccer team, the best-known team in County Wicklow. The players in the back row from left are: Shortt, Manley, Fortune, McKenna, Ivory and Kirwan. Front row: Kearney, Darcy, Hyland, Shortt, Kelly and Fortune.

Shamrock Boys' Soccer Team, **c. 1928**

The Shamrock Boys' Soccer Team of the 1927–8 season, winners of the Leinster Junior Cup.
(Left to right) Back: P. Doyle, T. Kelly, C. Byrne, J. Farrell and J. Windsor. Middle:
P. Kavanagh, J. O'Neill, B. Hyland, W. Scragg, P. Fitzgerald, C. Davis, T. Pluck and B. Brien.
Front: S. Hannon, E. Bellow, W. Byrne, D. Jordan, P. Doyle, D. Hannon and S. Brien.

Bray Golf Links, **c. 1910**

Some well-groomed gentlemen teeing off at Bray Golf Links. The links was established in
1896 on a site between Bray Bridge and the harbour. Bray Golf Club is reputed to be one
of the oldest golf clubs in the country. In 2003 it moved to a new location on the western
slope of Bray Head, on the Greystones Road.

Woodbrook Golf Club, **c. 1943**

The team of Woodbrook Golf Club players posing with the Barton Cup. (Left to right) Back: J. J. Doyle, P. Redmond, D. Lynch, J. A. McMahon, B. Lynch, M. McCarthy and C. J. McAllister. Front: Reverend C. Brady, J. D. O'Reilly, J. E. Kenny (Captain), B. J. Scannell and J. Moran.

Camogie, **c. 1928**

Members of the Bray Women's Camogie team.

Bray Emmets Banner, c. 1913

The Bray Emmets banner, featuring a portrait of Robert Emmet, was designed in 1887 for the club. In 1903 the Bray club paraded behind the banner during celebrations for Emmet in Dublin. Hundreds of other GAA clubs also paraded. The banner is now in the GAA Museum in Croke Park.

Bray Emmets GAA Club, c. 1901

Bray Emmets Club was founded in 1885. This is a photograph of the winning Senior Football Club League in 1901. (Left to right) Back: J. Garvey, W. Casey, T. O'Sullivan, J. Black, J. Ashford and J. Conron. Middle: H. Lyons, A. Dunne, P. Doyle, S. Mulvey, M. Byrne, W. Byrne, T. Duggan and N. Byrne. Front: J. J. Creegan, L. Flanagan, J. Cunningham, J. Dempsey, M. Cranley, T. Leggett and J. J. Clarke.

Matt Britton, c. 1952

Bray man Matt Britton had a long association with Bray Emmets and played hurling and handball with them. In later years he was a club and board official. He died in 1972 at the age of 98.

Bray Priest's Cup, c. 1931

The club members and officials who won the Bray Priest's Cup. Father D. O'Brien is seated in the centre.

Tour de France, 1998

In 1998 the Tour de France began outside mainland Europe for the first time. Ireland was chosen as the venue due to the high regard the race organisers had for the performances of Stephen Roche and Seán Kelly. One leg of the race commenced in Dublin and followed a gruelling course through Bray and over the Wicklow Mountains.

Sea Anglers, c. 1962
A group of Bray sea anglers stand proudly beside a trophy. The Bray Sea Anglers Club was established in 1960.

Bray Cove Swimming Club, c. 1944
Some junior members of the Bray Cove Swimming Club attend a swimming gala.

Poster, c. 1944

A poster advertises swimming and social events during the Annual Swimming Gala at the swimming pools, Bray Head.

Bray Wanderers, c. 1945

The Bray Wanderers Team of 1944–5 when they played in Division 3. (Left to right) Back: T. Tinan, V. Peters, L. McEvoy, J. Vance, L. Davis, H. Byrne, J. Lowe and J. Redmond. Front: T. Doyle, M. Cranley, D. Kelly and B. Keogh.

Bray Wanderers, c. 1950

The Bray Wanderers team of the 1950–51 season when they were winners of the FAI Junior Cup.

Bray Emmets, c. 1919
Members of the Bray Emmets GAA team of 1919 with club officials.

Bray Unknowns, c. 1922
The Bray Unknown Association Football team of 1922–3 having won the Metropolitan Cup. Also included in the photograph are club selectors and officials.

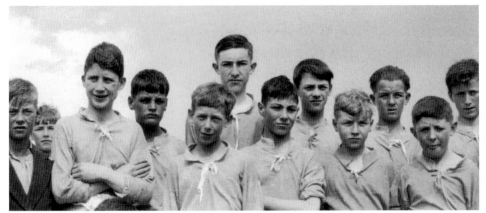

Bray Priest's Cup, c. 1932
Members of the successful team which won the Bray Priest's Cup competition. They are C. Ferguson, G. Reynolds, T. Doyle, M. Byrne, P. Mooney, S. Lyons, P. Murtagh, A. Cleary, T. Doyle, R. Britton and G. Ormonde.

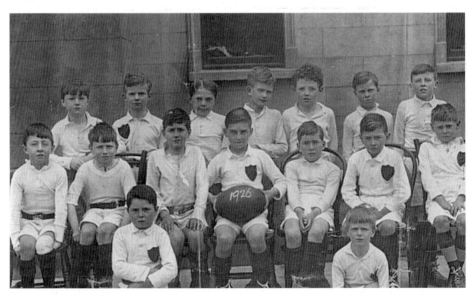

Under 10s, c. 1926
Presentation College, Under 10s Rugby team. (Left to right) Back: H. O'Carroll, T. Murphy, M. Murphy, O. Butler, J. Gilmartin, D. Ryan and D. Mooney. Middle: K. Doyle, G. Bailey, K. Blackwell, H. Lyons, B. Scannell, P. O'Brien and M. McCall. Front: J. O'Brien and G. Ellis.

Bray Golf Club, c. *1900*
Members of Bray Golf Club and their guests pose outside the pavilion.

Woodbrook Cricket Club, c. *1909*
Members of various Woodbrook Cricket teams pose before a marquee. The dog in the foreground appears out of place.

Well-known Faces, c. 1984
Some well-known Bray people who played on Centenary Day at Emmet Park.

6

Organisations

Coast Watchers, c. 1943

Members of the coast watch service that maintained an alert along the east coast during the
Emergency (1939–45).

Civil Defence, c. 1970
The Bray Civil Defence Casualty Service, County Competition winners 1970. (Left to right) Back: S. O'Toole, L. Mullally and D. Craney. Front: B. Stokes, G. Dowling and D. Coleman.

Catholic Boy Scouts, c. 1927
A happy group of scouts camping on Bray Head.

First Bray Sea Scouts, c. *1919*
Cubs and scouts of the First Bray Sea Scouts on camp with Reverend R. H. Cochran and Lord Powerscourt.

Bray Sea Scouts, c. *1928*
A troop of the First Bray Sea Scouts.

St Kevin's Pipe Band, **c. 1912**

St Kevin's Pipe Band shortly after their foundation. The band played at sporting events and gave regular recitals on the bandstand. For many decades they led the St Patrick's Day parade in the town.

St Kevin's Pipe Band, **c. 1930**

No parade or special event in Bray or the surrounding towns was complete without a performance by St Kevin's Pipe Band.

Old IRA Parade, c. 1950

The Sixth Battalion, Dublin Brigade, Old IRA commemorating the Easter Rising outside St Peter's Church, Little Bray. Amongst those in the photograph are D. Bennett, J. Owens, M. McGarry, S. Byrne, J. Fox and O. Gallagher.

FCA, c. 1993

An FCA squad marches past the Town Hall at the head of the St Patrick's Day parade.

Fianna Fáil Function, c. *1942*
A local Fianna Fáil function at the Royal Hotel. Centre back Dan Breen and Séamus Moore TD.

Post Office, c. *1950*
Postman Peter White beside his post office van outside Bray station. Six days a week he brought the late mail to the station to be transported to Dublin by train.

Convention, c. 1939

Some of the large contingent attending the ITGWU Annual Conference in Bray, 1939, pictured outside the Town Hall.

Fifth Wicklow Scouts, **c. 1987**
A gathering of cubs, beavers and scouts of the Fifth Wicklow Sea Scouts troop following the St Patrick's Day Parade.

Fifth Wicklow Scouts, **c. 1987**
Hi-jinks amongst some of the beavers of the Fifth Wicklow Sea Scouts.

Chamber of Commerce, c. 1981
Executive Council members and Directory Project members of Bray Chamber of Commerce at the launch of the Bray Directory. The Chamber of Commerce was founded in Bray in 1956.

Wolfe Tone Square, c. 1935
The official opening of Wolfe Tone Square Housing Scheme by the Minister for Local Government, Seán T. O'Kelly. Families were rehoused from condemned houses in Little Bray to this new housing scheme. Left to right: P. O'Brien, Father Brady, H. B. Hipwell, George Byrne, Seán T. O'Kelly, Peter Ledwidge, P. Devitt, Johnny Dunne, J. McCaul, P. Murphy and E. Byrne.

Bray Town Council, c. 1934

Members of Bray Town Council outside the Town Hall, prior to a council meeting. (Left to right) Back: H. P. Hipwell, J. Kinsella, Johnny Dunne, J. Murphy, Paddy Martin, George Heatley and P. Cooney. Middle: Peter Ledwidge, M. Staines and George Byrne. Front: J. Murphy (Town Engineer), J. J. Ryan, J. McCaul, James O'Brien, Edward Byrne, Miss Lavelle, P. Devitt and John Duffy.

7

Church and Education

Ravenswell Convent, c. 1950

The girls of First Class, Ravenswell Convent. The convent was run by the Sisters of Charity.

Ravenswell Convent, c. 1948
The boys and girls of Ravenswell Convent on a nature walk with their teacher, Miss Foley.

St Paul's School, c. *1950*
The pupils of St Paul's National School, Herbert Road, with their teacher.

Cripples Home, c. *1881*
The staff and children of Sunbeam House. This was a home founded in 1874 by Lucinda
Sullivan for destitute crippled children, then known as the Cripples Home.

Cripples Home, c. 1927
Children at play in the Cripples Home, Lower Dargle Road. There were many attempts to change the name of the institution, and finally 'Sunbeam House' was adopted. In 1957 they moved premises to the more spacious Glenmalure House on Vevay Road.

Kilmacanogue School, c. 1930
A group of happy children from Kilmacanogue National School.

Confirmation, c. 1952
The confirmation class of Presentation College, Bray.

First Holy Communion, c. 1949
Some First Holy Communion children of Ravenswell Convent with Canon Moriarity and their teacher Miss Braden.

Boys' School, c. 1928
Pupils of Big Bray Boys' National School, Brighton Terrace. In 1932 the school moved to new premises on Vevay Hill, to be known as St Cronan's National School.

Corpus Christi Procession, c. *1930*

For many decades up to the late 1960s one of the most important events in the Church's calendar was the annual Corpus Christi procession. Various groups lined up along Main Street and proceeded to a large field behind Loreto Convent where Mass was celebrated. In this photograph the girls from St Patrick's National School are in procession.

Loreto Convent, c. *1975*
This is a photograph of Loreto Convent and conservatory. In 1834 the conservatory was erected by the Putland family at Sans Souci. In 1850 the Loreto Sisters bought the house as a convent and boarding school.

St Patrick's Day Parade, **c. 1982**
The girls of St Patrick's National School taking part in the St Patrick's Day parade.

An Lár, **c. 1972**
Some of the younger children of Naíonra an Lár School, Bray, with their teacher. The school was established in Bray in 1971 by Craobh Chualann, Conradh na Gaeilge.

Father Twomey's Funeral, **c. 1946**

The town closed down for the funeral procession of Father Twomey. He had been a popular curate in the town for many years. The photograph shows the cortège passing down Main Street.

Tommy Kinsella, c. 1976

Reverend Canon Pigott, Parish Priest of the Church of the Most Holy Redeemer, congratulating Tommy Kinsella on being awarded the papal medal and certificate for sixty years' service to the church. Also present is Father John O'Connell who later became Parish Priest.

New Church, c. 1946

His Grace the Archbishop of Dublin, Dr Charles McQuaid, blessing the outer walls of the new Church of Our Lady, Queen of Peace.

New Church, **c. 1946**

The interior dedication ceremony at the opening of the Church of Our Lady, Queen of Peace.

Most Holy Redeemer, **c. 1946**

The wedding of Jim Tobin and Patricia Dunphy in the Church of the Most Holy Redeemer. The interior of the church has changed considerably since this photograph was taken. The altar rail and pulpit have been removed and there is an organ where the altar once stood.

Most Holy Redeemer, **c. 1907**

The exterior view of the Church of the Most Holy Redeemer, Main Street. The original church was built in 1826 and was enlarged in 1850. In later years the entire front of the church was changed.

Corpus Christi Procession, c. *1944*

The Men's Sodality preceded by a band. Note the segregation of the sexes; the women walked in procession with their own Sodalities.

Christ Church, c. *1910*

A horse and trap driving up Church Road, with the imposing edifice of Christ Church in the background. This was the leading Church of Ireland church in the town. The foundation stone was laid in 1861. William Gladstone, while on a visit to Bray in 1877, made a donation of £50 for a peal of bells.

The Bell Ringers, c. 1931

The bell ringers of Christ Church proudly display the award they won in a bell-ringing competition. (Left to right) Standing: Charles Lane, Wingfield Hall, David MacKenzie, Eric MacKenzie, Bob Harris, George Fennell, Cecil Hall, David Gibson, George Lane, Jack Fennell and Rodney MacKenzie. Seated: William Smith, Canon G. D. Scott, Jack Tough and Bob Simpson.

St Peter's Church, c. 1940

An interior view of St Peter's Roman Catholic Church, Little Bray. The church was built in 1837 as a replacement for the church at Crinken, which had fallen down. This small, unpretentious structure is hidden from the public road and built to the design of the Penal days.

St Peter's Church, c. 1956

The old burial ground behind the church, with headstones dating to the mid 1800s. In 1905 when all available space had been used for graves, adjoining land was purchased for the new cemetery.

Bishop Brendan Comiskey, c. 1981

In 1979 Bishop Brendan Comiskey came to live in Cluain Mhuire, Killarney Road, Bray, when he was appointed Bishop of Glendalough and Auxiliary Bishop of Dublin. In 1983 he was appointed Bishop of Ferns where he remained until he resigned in 2002. In this photograph he poses with four-year-old Damian Flynn.

Bishop Donal Murray, c. 1988
In 1983 Bishop Donal Murray was appointed as Bishop Comiskey's successor in Bray. In 1997 Bishop Murray was appointed Bishop of Limerick. Here he poses with Damian Flynn following his Confirmation in the Most Holy Redeemer.

St Paul's Church, c. 1907
The present St Paul's Church was erected in 1609. Since 1280 there had been an earlier church on this site when St Paul's was the centre of a rural deanery, called the Deanery of Bray. In 1862 the historian Reverend Canon George Scott was appointed rector there. In later years it closed and was turned into an organ factory.

Corpus Christi Procession, c. *1950*
Canon Moriarity carrying the monstrance past Duff's pub on Main Street, as local men
kneel in respect.

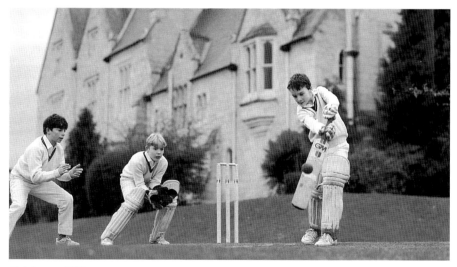

Cricket, c. *1988*
Three young boys play cricket in the grounds of Aravon School, a private school that
transferred to the Old Conna Hill Hotel in 1984. Old Conna House had previously been a
hotel and home of Count Cyril McCormack. The original Aravon was founded on Meath
Road in 1862 as a private day/boarding school. The most distinguished past pupils of the
school were Roger Casement and John Millington Synge.

Corpus Christi Procession, c. 1947

A group of children in their First Holy Communion and Confirmation dresses, in position outside Bells and Swastika Laundry, Main Street.

Altar Boys, c. 1985

A reunion of the long-serving altar boys of the Most Holy Redeemer Church with Parish Priest Father John O'Connell and Father McCarthy.

First Communion, c. *1988*

The First Holy Communion class of St Patrick's National School, Bray, with Sister Anna and Father John O'Connell.

Boys' School, c. *1916*

Some of the boys of Bray Boys' National School, which was then located at the rear of the Most Holy Redeemer Church. Note some of the boys with stiff white collars. The original school was founded in 1820 on Seapoint Road.

REGISTER OF RELIGIOUS INSTRUCTION.

Date of Visit 1893		Name of Clergyman	No. on Rolls	No. present	Have the Children Catechisms
March	3	L O'Byrne	255	174	yes
„	9	L O'Byrne	258	195	„
„	14	L O'Byrne	258	197	„
„	16th	Michael Hogan	258	162	„
„	20th	Michael Hogan	257	202	„
„	22nd	Michael Hogan	257	191	„
„	„	L O'Byrne	257	191	„
„	24th	Michael Hogan	257	156	„
April	10	L O'Byrne	258	177	„
„	11	L O'Byrne	259	185	
„	12th	Michael Hogan	259	180	
„	13th	Michael Hogan	259	180	„
„	17th	Michael Hogan	263	181	„
„	20	L O'Byrne	263	181	„
„	21	Michael Hogan	263	169	„
„	24th	Michael Hogan	263	198	„
„	25	L O'Byrne	263	197	„

School Register, c. *1893*

The register of religious instruction for Bray Boys' National School.

8

Personalities

James Whitecock, c. 1890

Whitecock was known as the Bard of Bray as he often wrote and played his own compositions around the Bray area. He was also the first assistant at the Bray Boys' National School in the 1880s.

Heritage Centre, c. 1985
The official opening of the Bray Heritage Centre at the Royal Hotel. (Left to right) Bray Lord Mayor Danny Bohan, Minister for Education Gemma Hussey, Centre Secretary Arthur Flynn, An Taoiseach Dr Garret FitzGerald, Centre Chairman Liz McManus, Chairman Cualann Historical Society Colm McCormack and Father Tony Deane.

Christy Brien, c. 1980
Christy worked as a butcher's porter for 35 years. His main interest was in local history and he assembled photographs and other material on all aspects of Bray. He also gave lectures and led historical walks. He was born in Bray in 1906 and died in 1986.

Presidential Visit, c. 1975

The President of Ireland, Cearbhall Ó Dálaigh, made an official visit to Bray to receive an honour from the Council and St Cronan's School. Ó Dálaigh was born on 12 February 1911 at number 85 Main Street, Bray. He was the second son of fish and poultry manager Richard Daly. He attended St Patrick's and St Cronan's National School. In 1974 he was inaugurated as the fifth President of Ireland. In 1976 he resigned in controversial circumstances and died in 1977.

Presidential Visit, c. 1975

Jim Molloy and Brother Clement greet President Ó Dálaigh as he attended a Bray Musical Society production at Presentation College.

Royal Visit, c. 1964

Prince Rainier and Princess Grace of Monaco during a visit to Powerscourt House to attend the Petite Ball. Members of the County Wicklow Civil Defence served as a Guard of Honour for the royal couple. (Left to right) Dermot Cranny, Eileen Cullen, Doreen O'Neill, M. O'Toole and G. O'Toole.

Seán Lemass, c. 1948

Seán Lemass was surrounded by well-wishers in Novara Grounds during an official visit to Bray. Amongst those present were (left to right) Mousy Murphy, Mrs Gaughran, Miss Temple, Bill Dutton, Bridgie Fox, Mona Carroll, Maggie Timmons, Mrs Brien and Mary O'Toole.

Bray Author, c. 1955

A youthful Peter Regan on a shopping trip with his mother Josephine. He is a well-loved author of many children's sports books set in Bray.

Literary Walk, c. 1997

As part of the Oscar Wilde Autumn School, the Bray Literary Walk is about to set off. During the course of the walk, members would see the homes of James Joyce, Oscar Wilde, Liam O'Flaherty and Neil Jordan.

Newspaper Seller, c. *1962*
The well-known newspaper seller Dan 'Chicken' Reilly who sold morning and evening papers at the Royal Corner for over forty years.

Bray Characters, c. *1986*
Some well-known Bray characters on their perch at the Wyvern statue outside the Town Hall. (Left to right) Back: Jack Carrig, Billy Reynolds and Jack Earles. Front: Dan 'Chicken' Reilly, Bartley Delaney and Peter Dawson.

Endeavour Awards, c. 1981

The Bray Endeavour Awards were organised annually by the Chamber of Commerce. The winners in 1981 were (left to right) Back: Gerry Casey, Syl Holland, Joe Maguire, Jim Molloy and Akis Courtellas. Front: Gemma Barry, Joe Duggan and Helen Clear.

Séamus Costello, c. 1972

Séamus Costello addressing a public meeting outside the Town Hall in Bray. He was born in Bray and at the age of 17 he joined the IRA. In 1957 he was interned for two years. He was elected as a Sinn Féin councillor to both Bray Urban District Council and Wicklow County Council. In 1974 he was expelled from Sinn Féin and was elected as an Independent Sinn Féin candidate. On 5 October 1977 he was assassinated while sitting in his car.

9

Films

Robert Mitchum, c. 1959

The Hollywood star Robert Mitchum in white shirt, with Irish actor Dan O'Herlihy, on location for the film 'A Terrible Beauty'. The film concerned IRA activities in the late 1940s, and was filmed in Ardmore Studios and on location in County Wicklow.

Filming, c. 1963

Laurence Harvey and Nanette Newman (at coach) with crew, filming 'Of Human Bondage' on location at the old gas works, behind the docks at Bray harbour. During the scene a steam train shunted on the tracks overhead.

Extras, c. 1995

A section of the 5,000 extras recruited for the Bloody Sunday sequence in the film 'Michael Collins', inside the Carlisle Grounds, Bray. The director of the film, Neil Jordan, lived in Bray for a number of years.

The Miracle, c. 1991

Extras on the set of 'The Miracle' which was being directed on Bray sea-front by Neil Jordan. The film, starring Donal McCann and Beverley D'Angelo, was a drama set in Bray.

Period Extras, c. 1993

A group of extras on the set of 'The Old Curiosity Shop' at Ardmore Studios.

On Location, c. *1997*

Shooting the assassination scene in the film 'The General' at Herbert Road, Bray. In the centre behind the stretcher is a bloodstained Brendan Gleeson who played Martin Cahill, the General of the title.

Ballykissangel, c. *1998*

The cast and crew of the popular BBC television series 'Ballykissangel', on location at Sidmonton Square, Bray.

Young Cassidy, c. 1964
Actor Rod Taylor on location for the film 'Young Cassidy'. The film traced the early life of the Dublin playwright Sean O'Casey. John Ford, the original director, had to retire from the project when he fell ill and Jack Cardiff finished the film.

Medieval Film, c. 2002
A group of colourful extras on the set of the big-budget film 'Ella Enchanted' at Ardmore Studios. This fantasy film was shot on elaborate sets at the studio and starred Anne Hathaway, Hugh Dancy and Joanna Lumley.

Ardmore Studio, c. 1980
One of the workshops in Ardmore Studios. A craftsman puts the finishing touches to a prop. The large head in the background was used in the film 'Zardoz'.

Jack and Fred, c. 1976
An Taoiseach Jack Lynch enjoys a drink with Charlotte Rampling and Fred Astaire during a visit to Ardmore Studios. The two stars were then filming 'The Purple Taxi'.

Morgan O'Sullivan, c. 1977

The producer Morgan O'Sullivan relaxing at his desk in Ardmore Studios. O'Sullivan was born and lives in Bray and has been co-producer on many of the big-budget films produced in Ireland, including 'Braveheart' and 'Reign of Fire'.

Extras Wanted, c. 1995

This was the poster that appeared throughout counties Wicklow and Dublin seeking free extras for the film 'Michael Collins'. Director Neil Jordan sought 5,000 male extras to recreate the Bloody Sunday massacre of 1920. Over 5,000 people answered the call and the dramatic scene was shot in one take with five cameras.

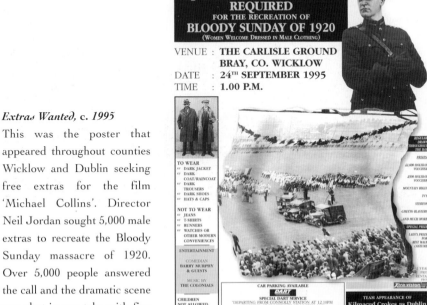

10

Tourism

Touring Group, c. 1947

The touring group Funzapoppin, one of the many fit-ups that visited Bray between the 1940s and 60s. From left: Danny Cummins, Mickser Reid, Frank O'Donovan and Hal Roach. The advent of television was to see the demise of this form of live entertainment. Other groups to visit Bray regularly were the George Daniels and the McFaddens Road Shows.

International Hotel, **c. 1966**

In 1865 John Brennan built the International Hotel opposite the railway station at a cost of £24,000. It was the largest hotel in the town and a popular rendezvous at weekends for dancing and social events. During the First World War it was temporarily converted into the Princess Patricia Hospital for wounded soldiers. In 1974 the hotel was destroyed by fire and had to be demolished.

Old Conna Hill Hotel, **c. 1966**

Sir Charles Lanyon designed the original Old Conna House as a magnificent residence. In the 1950s it was owned by Count Cyril McCormack, who ran it as an upmarket hotel. In 1984 Aravon School relocated here.

BRESLIN'S

ROYAL MARINE HOTEL,

BRAY,

Is a first-class Establishment. It is situated on the beach, and contiguous to the Railway Terminus. The prospects embrace a wide range of sea and mountain.

Royal Marine Hotel, c. 1870

Following the introduction of the railway to Bray in 1854, many hotels were erected to accommodate the growing number of visitors. The Royal Marine Hotel was one such, built adjacent to the station by Edward Breslin. On 22 August 1916 the hotel was destroyed by fire.

Bray Head Hotel, c. 1950

The Bray Head Hotel enjoys a wonderful location at the northern end of the promenade, at the base of Bray Head. The hotel was built in 1862 by John Lacey and is still in business today.

The Eagle's Nest, c. 1956

A summer view of the Eagle's Nest Café. The Veranda Café was located midway up the southern slope of Bray Head. From the café diners could enjoy panoramic views of the coastline as far as Howth. At night the venue became a ballroom.

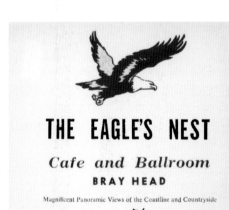

The Eagle's Nest, c. 1956

An advertisement for The Eagle's Nest Café and Ballroom. With the introduction of the aerial chair-lift in 1952, the journey to and from the venue became more enjoyable.

Bar B, c. 1950

This advertisement for the famous Bar B ballroom at Woodbrook promotes Johnny Butler and his orchestra, one of the favourite bands to play there. Every weekend special buses brought thousands of dancers there from Dublin, Dun Laoghaire and the surrounding areas.

* * *

BILLY CARTER.

Dance-Band Leader at the Arcadia (attached to the International Hotel, Bray). This justly popular musician sets thousands of dancing feet tingling to the rhythm of his famous band.   His fans say : " Bray would not be Bray without him."

* * *

Billy Carter, c. 1958

Adjoining the International Hotel was the Arcadia Ballroom, one of the largest dancing arenas in the country. Billy Carter was one of the favourite dance-band leaders to play at the venue. In the 1960s all the leading showbands from the Royal to the Miami played there. Many big names including Roy Orbison and Acker Bilk played dates at the Arcadia. In 1962 it was destroyed by fire.

Toft's Amusements, c. 1935

Two women at Toft's Amusements, one of the many amusements along the sea-front. Dodgems, ghost trains, hall of mirrors, swinging boats and chairoplanes were popular with young and old alike.

Fossetts Circus, c. 1990
A happy group with the Strong Man outside Fossetts Circus. Children eagerly looked forward to the annual visits by Fossetts and Duffy's Circuses.

Holidays in Bray, c. 1918
Advertisements for the International Hotel, Bray Head Hotel and Marine Station Hotel which appeared in a tourist brochure. It was important to emphasise the nearness to the sea and also the proximity to Kingstown (later Dun Laoghaire) as many of the guests travelled by boat from England.

11

Floods

Sheridan's Lane Flood, c. 1905

On 26 August 1905 the Dargle River burst its banks, unleashing a devastating flood on these single-storey homes. In the photograph children wade through the water while others inspect the damage.

Carriage, **c. 1905**

An abandoned carriage on 25 August 1905 gives an indication of the depth of the water which engulfed the Little Bray area. In the background is the tower of Little Bray Castle.

Dargle Road Flood, **c. 1946**

One of the regular floods on Lower Dargle Road. This one occurred on 12 August 1946 when the Dargle River burst its banks. The flood did not prevent local men Séamus O'Dowd and Seán Fox going about their business.

Dublin Road Flood,* c. *1965
The freak flood of July 1965 caused havoc to traffic on the Dublin Road. Here a bus negotiates the flood water.

Hurricane Charlie, 1986
Another victim of Hurricane Charlie on the night of 24 August 1986. This tree at Bray Head was completely uprooted.

Sea Power, **c.** *1992*
A heavy sea lashing the promenade during spring tides. Martello Terrace in the background was built in 1861. From 1887 the young James Joyce lived at number 1 with his family for four years. Later residents have included the film director Neil Jordan, singer Mary Coughlan and Liz McManus TD.

Big Snow, 1982
The Big Snow of 1982 which brought the east coast to a standstill. The photograph shows the snowbound, newly-built Rosslyn Estate following the blizzard. In the background is Christ Church.

12

Transport

Dublin to Bray Train, c. 1928

Three steam engines in Bray station. These engines were built in Grand Canal Street in the early 1900s for the Dublin South East Railway. The steam trains were taken out of service c. 1957.

Drumm Train, c. 1940

Professor James Drumm initiated the Drumm train, a unique form of transport powered by electric batteries. In 1932 the train went into service on the Dublin–Bray line. It proved an effective service during the Emergency years of 1939–45 when there was a scarcity of fuels. The train continued in service until 1950.

Railway Staff, c. 1950

Staff at Bray Railway Station pose on the platform.

Train, c. 1956

A diesel train (or rail car) leaving Bray Station for Dublin. The first diesel trains went into service on the Bray to Harcourt Street line. Later they were introduced on the Bray to Westland Row line. In the background is the International Hotel.

Traffic, c. 1952

Traffic on Quinsboro Road. Note the bus in the foreground and the bicycles parked by the kerb. Thankfully, this streetscape retains most of its character half a century later.

Sea-front Road Train, c. 1999

The latest form of transport to hit Bray — the Sea-front Road Train. This colourful train travels along the promenade and back along the road to the circular area at the base of Bray Head.

Railway Station, c. 1945

The engine of the Rosslare to Dublin steam train on the right of the picture has just completed filling up with water in Bray Station. Note the water tank to the right of the engine.

13

Street Scenes

Main Street, c. 1890

Note the absence of traffic at what is now a very busy junction, where Herbert Road meets Main Street and Quinsboro Road. Quin's Hotel (later the Royal Hotel) is on the left corner.

Main Street, **c. 1930**

The architecture of the upper floors of the buildings has changed little in the 70 years or so. In this era most of the men wore headgear, and bicycles were very much in vogue.

The Bridge below the Town, **c. 1940**

There has been a bridge over the Dargle River at this location since 1666. In 1741 this bridge was washed away in a storm. The present bridge was designed by David Edge and erected in 1856.

The Bridge, c. 1940

The bridge has always been a favourite meeting-place for men. Here the unemployed or elderly would gather to discuss the problems of the world. Others would fish or watch the path of salmon proceeding up river to spawn.

Dargle River, c. 1940

A photograph of the Dargle taken from the People's Park at low tide. The river could be a source of joy to children paddling and catching minnows, and to poachers who made a lucrative trade in catching salmon.

River Wall, c. *1935*
Four young people sitting on the river wall with the old mill in the background. From left:
John Byrne, Tiny Bowden, Sheila Bowden and Tom Swan.

Bray Men, c. *1925*
Some Bray men enjoy the sun on one of the most sought-after seats in town, outside the
Boat House on the sea-front.

Roxy Cinema, c. 1949
Three young girls, Irene 12, Muriel five and Patricia 10, outside the Roxy Cinema, Albert Avenue, one of the three cinemas in town. The other cinemas were Macs in the old Turkish Baths, and the Royal Cinema, now a Cineplex.

Bray Women, c. 1948
Women residents of Maitland Street in Little Bray pose happily for a photograph. From left: Mrs Finnegan, Mrs McCabe, Mrs Byrne, (?), Mrs Ivory, Mrs Byrne, Mrs McCarthy, Mrs Windsor, Mrs McCarthy and Mrs Byrne.

Celebrating, c. 1929
Residents of a cottage in Little Bray celebrate the Catholic Emancipation Centenary.

Town Hall, c. 1995
The Town Hall, built by Lord Meath as a market house in 1881, underwent major renovations in the 1980s. The ground floor was refurbished as a restaurant and, despite much local protest, is now a McDonald's fast-food outlet.

Esplanade Terrace, **c. 1985**

Sir William Wilde built numbers 1–4 Esplanade Terrace in the 1860s. The family sojourned here regularly. The playwright Oscar Wilde spent summer holidays in Bray. When a sexual scandal broke involving Sir William, the family took refuge in Bray.